For Denise Marin, my partner for 43 years and the love of my life. And to my children, Anna, John and Ariel, my heartfelt gratitude for the joy and encouragement you have given me.

Client Testimonials

"MarketCues' SmartPlan360° Program was invaluable in assessing our organizational performance. It provided us with a qualified set of metrics to measure and better manage our leadership and products. Any organization would be well served by this program."

Dr. Eric Roe, Executive Director
Texas Engineering Executive Education
The University of Texas at Austin

"I hired MarketCues because my agency had become stagnant. They analyzed my business and provided a clear strategy forward. One year later, we'd grown by 40%. Having an expert like Tom by my side has made every bit of a difference."

Robert Wurzel, Chief Executive Officer
The Wurzel Insurance Agency

"We thought that we could handle our marketing needs in-house and that we had a pretty creative team. We quickly learned that MarketCues' expertise could help us cultivate the image we've been trying to achieve for years. Although we're not MarketCues' largest client, they always treat us like we are."

Angie Romagosa, President/CEO
The Sharing Center

"MarketCues gave us critical business information based on research and interviews with our closest strategic partners and clients. The approach brought together many divergent viewpoints into one potent strategic initiative."

Jerry Ross, Executive Director
National Entrepreneur Center

"We hired MarketCues to assist us with a major corporate and brand marketing program. With their help, we renamed our company, repositioned ourselves, and created a new identity and all necessary marketing resources. Their work is excellent."

Ola Williams, CEO
Bell Performance

"MarketCues' 360° Church Program has been an answer to our prayers! It has allowed us more time to focus on our ministry rather than try to sort through development issues. I highly recommend this comp any to churches of any size."

Ron Lewis, Senior Minister
King's Park, Durham, NC and
Every Nation NYC, New York

"We searched for a firm that would understand our work in film, animation and publishing. MarketCues brought us all of that and more."

Tim and Candice Argall, Founders
Adventures of Toby/Bugbox

"Working with MarketCues is like having a partner who cares as much about your business as you do."

Farrel Crowder, CEO
Crowder Corporation

This book is available for special discounts for bulk purchases for sales
promotions or premiums. Special editions, including personalized covers,
excerpts of existing books, and corporate imprints, can be created in large
quantities for special needs. For more information, write to MarketCues,
Inc., 8311 Brier Creek Parkway, Suite 105-522, Raleigh, NC 27617
or email info@marketcues.com.

Library of Congress Catalog in-Publication Data

Marin, Tom.
Rethink / Tom Marin. 1st edition:
Management Consulting Services.
Business Consulting Services.
MarketCues—company.

ISBN-13: 978-1727138641
ISBN-10: 1727138643

Printed in the United States of America

Design by Joshua Bowens

| **Contents**

| Introduction

The Four Drivers of Smart Organizational Strategy

This book is the result of 30 years' work. Not the writing –– that only took about a year –– but the day-in, day-out of three decades as a consultant for companies and non-profits of all sizes.

I've learned a lot from my clients. Analyzing their organizations, listening to the way they described everything from operations and market share to staffing and deadlines, I learned that despite the best intentions of top executives, many organizations simply do not have a workable, smart organizational strategy in place to achieve their stated goals.

It all begins with a leader's willingness to make an honest appraisal of the organization's strengths and weaknesses, and compare it with input from those they serve. Recognizing the difference between those assessments can jump-start the process. But building a healthy organization doesn't happen in a vacuum, with only senior leaders focused on the challenges. A healthy organization requires all employees to be fully engaged and energized.

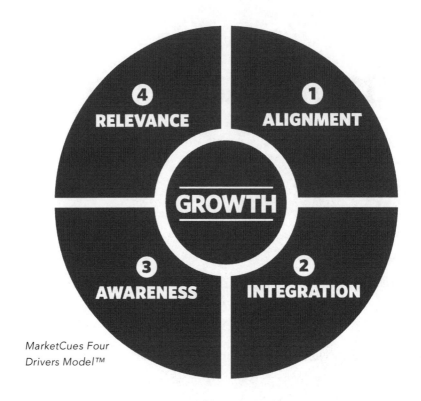

*MarketCues Four
Drivers Model™*

In the following chapters, I will discuss these four primary drivers for organizational health and growth:

Driver 1: RETHINK Your Organization's Alignment

Alignment of purpose points all departments in the same direction, and enables better service to customers. An organization that is not aligned internally will not be aligned externally with those it serves. A fully aligned organization says what it is going to do, and delivers.

Driver 2: RETHINK Your Organization's Integration

Every organization that seeks high performance

needs integration of purpose and action. All too often organizations have a set of stated goals and strategies but lack the culture to implement them. This can lead to a "Putting out the fires" mentality.

Driver 3: RETHINK Your Organization's Awareness

An organization needs to build and maintain awareness of its goals and values among employees and customers. This will take time if an organization has been functioning in silos for years.

Driver 4: RETHINK Your Organization's Relevance

Once an organization is aligned and integrated, with a high degree of awareness of its goals and values, it can focus on market relevance. Only a solidly built organization can deliver programs, products and services that will thrive in the marketplace.

In order to get ahead you have to think ahead. And you have to be willing to rethink everything. It takes work. Let's get started.

Driver 1:
RETHINK YOUR ORGANIZATION'S ALIGNMENT

TO rethink an organization's alignment, the leadership team must be willing to honestly assess its employees, processes and systems. These factors along with many related marketplace issues all impact an organization's alignment. The need for a fully aligned organization is compounded by today's fast-paced marketplace, where rapid change is the standard.

There are no shortcuts to success. All market sectors are being impacted, and many need to consider major transformations in response to new demands. For example, online education has opened up new markets and has also created an environment that all educational institutions must address to remain relevant.

In addition, there are nearly 75 million millennials worldwide, representing the largest living generation. Millennials have a combined purchasing power of over $10 trillion. They are fast becoming decision-makers at major corporations and nonprofits, including churches. For instance, many Senior Pastors are now under the age of 35, which was not the case as recently as the 1990s.

Technology is the primary tool used to launch new products, online instruction, advertising and book events. And it is a major factor in determining the productivity and profitability of organizations of all sizes and at all stages of maturity. For the millennial and baby-boom generations, purchases have shifted to online from traditional brick-and-mortar businesses. This has changed how people interact with goods and service providers, as well as how they make purchases.

An organization that has not aligned itself to these realities has little chance to stay current. This change is both exciting and challenging.

A great deal of time is spent in meetings clarifying what was said previously, why they said it, and what should be done next. An aligned organization will have many fewer of these kinds of meetings, since its true purpose is well known up and down the leadership team. And all those hours not spent in meetings is time staff can work on developing smart next steps.

What we're actually talking about here follows the rules of basic time management. If you know where you are going, and you've been there before, you'll arrive a lot faster than someone traveling an unfamiliar route. Organizational alignment provides everyone with the market intelligence needed to make smart strategic decisions that lead to continuous improvement and growth.

Based on an intensive study of over 500 organizations across multiple industries and geographies, we have identified four types of behavior that increase organizational alignment. We first identified these behaviors among highly successful organizations. We will discuss each behavior in the pages ahead:

Behavior 1: Roles, Responsibilities and Accountabilities

Behavior 2: High Performance Leadership Team

Behavior 3: Integrated Information Systems

Behavior 4: Financial Management and Transparency

Organizational alignment is often the missing ingredient that prevents an otherwise healthy organization from achieving its goals. Even an organization with a clear set of goals defined by senior leadership will come to a grinding halt if those goals are not widely understood by all employees. Even an organization with excellent products and services. Alignment really is the secret sauce.

Behavior 1: Roles, Responsibilities & Accountabilities

When an entire organization operates with a singularity of purpose, employees enjoy working together as a team. Our research shows that the great majority of organizations with high performing staff are the result of a leadership team that established a clear set of roles and accountabilities for everyone. And each employee understands why his or her role is important to the organization's success. Answering the "why" questions along the way is critical to motivating staff. Merely issuing orders does not produce the long-lasting teamwork all organizations strive to develop.

In every organization, input, direction, oversight and governance come down from the top. While that might sound obvious, the reality in many organizations is muddled. As an organization grows, it's crucial that each department has a clearly defined role, with responsibilities and accountabilities mapped out in detail. Team members' responsibilities must also be refined so that expectations are clearly understood.

For best results, an organizational chart should always be kept current. In a high-functioning organization, each employee understands his or her responsibilities, and is likely to be motivated to advance as positive results are achieved. This operates as a self-fulfilling prophecy: The more you achieve, the more you seek greater responsibility.

When we interview a new client's leaders and staff, we often receive varying definitions of the responsibilities of their given position. While leaders tend to describe one set of goals and responsibilities associated with a particular position, the staffer may paint a very different picture of what he or she actually does each day. The discrepancy is caused by the leadership team's lack of clarity. And it can slow things down. Staff members who understand what's expected of them will be empowered to seek and resolve problems at their level with less supervisory guidance. Staff members with only a fuzzy understanding of their role and responsibilities will take more time to get less done.

Case Study:
INDUSTRIAL CORPORATION WITH HIGH SUSTAINABILITY AND LOW SCALABILITY SCORES

I consulted with the CEO of an industrial corporation with approximately $12 million in annual revenues. This company had grown from a startup to a fairly healthy organization using its cash flow and an asset-based instrument. By all accounts, the CEO of this privately held corporation had much to celebrate, but sales growth had stalled and top management couldn't figure out why. The CEO engaged our firm to assess the base problem and provide strategic solutions to jumpstart revenues.

We started with product quality, sales expertise, and overall customer satisfaction. We found that the company offered the highest level of products and service of any in its industry. Once our organizational 360° showed that they had the technical know-how and willingness to service its clients we could appreciate the CEO's frustrations!

We then turned our attention to the corporation's organizational structure and determined it was still using the first stage of growth management – a centralized form of management where a few senior leaders were making all important decisions with zero input from their team members. On the surface this appeared to be a smart form of leadership: thin and lean. Centralized purchasing led to discounted vendor pricing and made project tracking easy.

That was fine when the corporation's clients were all located within a few time zones in North America. However, the corporation had grown significantly from its beginnings, and was currently serving clients on three continents and in several languages. This rapid, diversified growth had actually stalled growth and placed enormous pressure on all employees. And it explained why the corporation's sustainability score was high but its scalability score was low.

The strategic solution was to re-organize the corporation around a Geo-Divisional Structure. Industry experts were recruited in the locations served by the company, to provide direct assistance to customers and potential customers, and to increase business development. This new organizational structure included a cloud-based solution that integrated the company's communications with clients to ensure timely responses to every request.

After the new organizational structure had been fully implemented, the CEO reported that our approach had provided a fresh look at the company and a path to continued growth. Several years later the CEO let us know that annual revenues had increased 40% through leveraging the new organizational structure.

When roles and responsibilities are clearly understood throughout an entire organization, leaders will only need to reinforce them during meetings and at other opportune times. The organizations we've researched that take the time to explain why they are using specific processes and systems, and encourage positive behavior that is consistent with its cultural values, are thriving.

This type of leadership systematically eliminates roadblocks for staff. Clarity of purpose fosters a "solve it" mindset that does not seek blame, only solutions, and thereby encourages everyone's participation.

Behavior 2: High Performance Leadership Team

A high performance leadership team knows how to get things done. It implements a comprehensive staff development process that is well documented and easy to understand. For example, staff might be encouraged to receive continuing education, even if it is not directly related to their jobs. Tuition reimbursement provided by the organization would encourage this option. As a result, employees become motivated to work toward more challenging career paths.

Effective leaders clearly communicate what is expected of staff and what constitutes "success versus failure." This type of leadership has an effective quality-management system in place that keeps the organization healthy and on a growth curve. It accomplishes this by systematically providing training for Professional Development and Performance Leadership throughout all levels of the organization — not just in the executive suite. By reinforcing its commitment to each staff member, leaders encourage everyone to be proactive using his or her best judgment on behalf of the organization.

A major finding by the international research firm, Gallop, found that millennials want coaches, not bosses. When millennials quit jobs, it's often because of the boss, not the organization. I have observed this situation many times. The most common reasons given by an employee leaving a job included one or more of the following:

- Supervisor provided conflicting directions
- Supervisor micro-managed
- Supervisor created competitive conflicts among staff
- Supervisor acted like the expert on everything, leaving little room for input by anyone else
- Supervisor didn't seem to care whether the organization succeeded

As we further researched these kinds of exit statements, we were surprised to find that in nearly every case, the majority of the problems that caused employees to quit were due to a supervisor's attitude and behavior, not a team member's. And yet the majority of those problems led to the team member leaving the organization, rather than the supervisor. This type of supervisor, left unchecked, has the authority to destroy an entire department, division or even an organization depending upon their level of management.

Also, when there is little or no support from senior management, staff is likely to work at a "just enough" level. It's the law of reciprocity at work: I'll give you what you give me, and no more. It's unfortunate that senior leaders sometimes accept this behavior, either because it's ingrained, or because they aren't willing to change their own behavior and policies. That is a recipe for stagnation, or failure.

CASE STUDY:
PROFESSIONAL SERVICES CORPORATION DRIVES NEW GROWTH

A successful professional services corporation with a solid P/L and Balance Sheet was suffering due to stalled growth. The organization had been in business for three generations, so they were quite aware of how to manage its profitability. They had tried several strategies and marketing programs that enhanced their overall market identity and image, but none of those strategies raised their annual revenues. They wanted to try something different.

We conducted our Organizational 360° program using a three-phase approach: 1) Assessment of the organization and its customers in the markets served; 2) Prioritized strategic initiatives to drive growth given present resources; 3) Implemented 12 "Success Touch Points" to expand the company's strongest growth areas.

Throughout our work, the CEO accepted all of our strategic recommendations and quickly put them into action. There was absolutely no conflict in our discussions, despite our presenting negative aspects of his company's structure and processes. In fact, he seemed relieved to hear our critique.

As our relationship grew, I mentioned his quick response to our recommendations, letting him know that others I'd worked with had responded differently. He laughed and said he was only interested in accomplishing the goals he'd stated at the outset. "I'm just doing my job," he said.

He was surprised when I told him that I rarely heard such a statement from a leader in his position. After decades as a consultant, I can honestly say this was one of the most refreshing points of view I had experienced. I've worked with countless senior leaders who have trouble hearing anything but good news. And that makes them resistant to change. This clear-eyed CEO checked his ego at the door – and significantly raised his company's revenues.

Performance management is a strategic and integrated process. This is true for leadership and staff. Strong teams work toward maximizing the capabilities and skills of everyone in the organization. The end goal is a sense of partnership between leaders and team members as they work together to accomplish shared goals. There is no "them" versus "us" thinking.

Here are five steps to create a high-performance leadership team:

1. Define your organization's goals, objectives and tactics.

2. Create a performance management chart.

3. Create an action plan to achieve your goals, objectives and tactics.

4. Create guidelines for performance leadership coaching.

5. Practice conducting a performance interview with 3 role-players: Manager, Employee, and Observer.

Behavior 3: Integrated Information Systems

Organizations that can easily share all types of information among staff and those it serves are the best communicators. This requires ongoing staff training, and strong customer service and online support. With these mechanisms in place, an organization can identify challenges at early stages, before they become critical issues. Using this strategy promotes and enhances alignment.

Another important element of integrated information systems is making corrective actions visible to everyone, so that all staff can learn from each occurrence. A sharing philosophy produces an agile and flexible organization that preserves its core values and overcomes challenges as they occur. And it encourages the kind of free-form thinking that can give rise to solutions to problems before they surface. Managers who are willing to set up systems that facilitate everyone's awareness of corrective actions can get a leg up on their market's "next big thing." The more employees engage in a company's growth and well-being, the more likely that company is to succeed.

One key to setting up an effective information-sharing system is to design it with a 24/7 access capability. When quick response and corrective measures are available for most problems, employees will be motivated to participate. And consider using monthly reports to congratulate those who make use of the system. This helps create an aligned organization with highly motivated employees.

Most employees want to be an integral part of their organization. Simply having a job to earn pay is no longer an attractive career choice, particularly not for the millions of millennials in the workforce. For them, making a significant contribution is a key requirement to remaining motivated and focused. This is why organizations that want to attract talented staff need to understand the importance of staff development, and explore new ideas and mechanisms that support all employees. When an organization becomes more agile as a business, with everyone working toward the same goal, everyone benefits.

CASE STUDY:

FROM NON-PROFIT STARTUP
TO NATIONAL ORGANIZATION

The founder of a startup asked me to consult on best practices for building his nonprofit. I met with him and his wife in their home, along with their three volunteers. This was a bootstrap organization: No frills, no budget, just a desire to tackle worldwide hunger – and the hardened grit I've noted in the best business leaders.

Our starting point was integrating the nonprofit's communications and operations. From Day One, all our work would be accomplished online, using apps and a website. No printed materials were planned. The total commitment to digital communications solved one problem common to nonprofits, especially in their early stages: controlling costs.

The five people I sat with at that kitchen table had all come from large corporations that handled finance, marketing, human resources, and many other departments. And here they were planning to launch a nonprofit with activists from around the country, all of whom would be led by digital communications from the founder's desktop.

Ten years after that first meeting, the nonprofit is going strong. They are implementing grass-roots sustainability goals to reduce the carbon footprint, and helping communities create self-sufficient programs that feed those in need. Although I didn't ask for compensation, I've been well paid by the deep satisfaction I've felt watching them succeed and grow.

Behavior 4: Financial Management & Transparency

Establishing a standard of excellence for financial management and transparency provides an organization with a better experience for staff and among those the organization serves. To accomplish this, benchmarks are essential to exercise proper control and stewardship over finances and related operations. Financial management and transparency allows the organization to allocate resources more effectively by understanding what the organization's top priorities are, and which areas require more resources for further development and improvement.

An organization that has built a nimble financial management system can effortlessly produce a P/L and Balance Sheet and related financial reports by the fifth of the following month, and make them available to the entire organization. I realize this is an uncommon business practice, particularly among privately held firms. The major drawback with concealed or tightly controlled financials is that it breeds mistrust within an organization.

CASE STUDY:
IMPROPER USE OF FINANCIAL REPORTING

Sad to say, in three decades as a consultant, I have repeatedly witnessed inappropriate use of financial reporting by business leaders. While the majority of organizations I've had the opportunity to work with play by the rules of financial disclosures and reporting, inappropriate use of financials is by no means uncommon.

For example, I worked with a medium-size organization whose founder and president would not share an ounce of financial information with top leaders – except when sales fell below projections. Then suddenly, from seemingly nowhere, financial data was unleashed to support the president's anger at senior leaders he felt were "incompetent." To make a bad situation even worse, the president would also provide the damning data to staff, who could only feel bad about the situation, as they were in no position to do anything to help.

How much better it would have been if the president had provided financial information in a continuous flow – and allowed senior leaders to make course-corrections.

Of course, publicly traded companies are legally required to report their financial results, which keeps employees, shareholders and the business press in the know. However grudgingly some corporations and nonprofits may follow the laws, the upside of those regulations is that every employee can see the successes black and white, and when there are financial challenges ahead, motivated employees can help find solutions to them. Though few privately held firms are comfortable sharing financials with employees, most would find tremendous value implementing transparency as a best practice.

The following eight guidelines can be used to achieve financial transparency:

1. Establish a timeline of reporting for review.
2. Review your system for determining total monthly and annual financial performance, and compare it to the previous year's financials.
3. Ensure appropriate controls are in place and functioning.
4. Ensure transparency in financial reporting through online access.
5. Determine ratios between costs to services.
6. Find ways to reduce direct and indirect costs.
7. Find ways to increase delivery efficiency to meet the expectations of those served.

8. Share the results throughout the organization.

Sharing financial assessments with staff through scheduled reviews creates an atmosphere of teamwork and problem-solving (or celebrating). And it helps an organization stay aligned with its primary goals.

Savvy organizations know how to execute their formal financial plan as part of an overall "Balanced Scorecard" to achieve strategic goals. They know how to track and analyze variances against budget, and quickly identify whether they are achieving projected margins and where improvements can be made.

Many people think of a financial plan as little more than a roadmap with a heavy dose of fund-raising pit stops. These activities certainly occupy important functions in the life of an organization, but a good plan can serve a far larger purpose: It can reveal what your customers truly want from your organization based on their purchases or services used. And that can save you the time spent experimenting with new products or services — wasting precious resources in the process. It's also a useful barometer of your success rate, and it holds you accountable to your goals.

A client once told me that he didn't want to ask his customers for their feedback because he feared that if they thought too much about his company they might not want to continue with him. I encouraged him to put aside negative thinking and start listening to what his customers had to say. I explained that what he didn't know might hurt his business, so it was far better to be informed by their input, and make adjustments if necessary.

According to a report by the consulting firm Deloitte, since 1970, the average life expectancy of a Fortune 500 company has declined from around 75 years to less than 15 years today. Deloitte shows the topple rate (the rate at which companies change ranks) increasing as competition exposed low performers and ate away at their returns.

Economy-wide Firm Topple Rate (1965-2012)

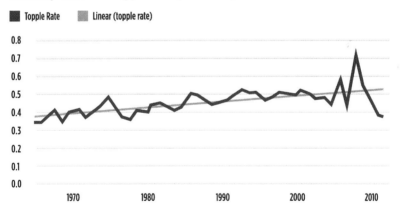

Source: Thomas C. Powell and Ingo Reinhardt

Not even tech Giant Google is immune; Three years after it bought Motorola for $12.5 billion, it off-loaded its new toy for a mere $3 billion. When you consider the fast pace of high-stakes poker being played in the corporate world's top ranks, you begin to understand why so many corporations find themselves in trouble now.

Businesses often fail when they are run as if they don't need to re-evaluate their strategies, or when they put self-interest before their customer's interests. Such behaviors create internal operations that are insulated from marketplace realities. And over time, their competition will leapfrog ahead through innovation.

Blockbuster, Kodak and Circuit City were once highly successful organizations, and yet they went out of business because they didn't pay attention to a changing marketplace. My work for FujiFilm gave me a front row seat into Kodak's mindset. At the time that FujiFilm was my client, Kodak had the digital chip that would be used in all digital cameras many years in the future. Yet Kodak held that chip in secrecy for a decade, because it didn't want the world of digital photography to interrupt or erode their long-standing film business.

That's an example of a leading firm undermining everything it worked so long and hard to build. Kodak's goal was financial superiority, but their lack of transparency, coupled with their insularity from a changing marketplace, led to catastrophic losses.

Chapter Summary

Effective leaders see their organization as one cohesive whole, not as individual parts working toward unique objectives. A fully aligned organization has:

- Leaders who have aligned their goals and mission to the roles, responsibilities and accountabilities throughout their organization.

- Leaders who use positive motivation strategies to create an engaging environment that drives high-performance work at all levels.

- Leaders who have integrated their information systems so all team members can make informed choices without direct supervision.

- Leaders who build transparency into their communications and reporting, so data is available to a staff filled with self-starters.

During the next chapter, RETHINK Your Organization's Integration, we will explore how successful leaders create stronger, more cohesive leaders and team members and how they leverage this integration with their customers.

Driver 2:
RETHINK YOUR ORGANIZATION'S INTEGRATION

ORGANIZATIONAL integration is the process of implementing a well-defined — and aligned — set of goals, values and operations. Organizations without strong integration cannot execute plans in an effective manner. It can neither make quick decisions nor deliver on them. And that will inevitably lead to business or membership losses.

Timing is everything in so many internal decisions. As a result, organizations that can confidently choose productive directions will deliver faster, better results. Integration produces decisions that are based on aligned purposes and values. When all team members know what should be done for a best outcome, decisions flow naturally.

Implementing integration throughout an organization keeps everyone informed and up-to-date with critical information needed to serve the common goal. And integration increases an organization's ability to respond to external changes, such as economic factors, technological advances, and political and cultural shifts — all factors a nimble organization can address. An organization that is not aware of these dynamics, or is aware of them but unable to quickly and easily respond to them, will lose market share.

Integrating departments and systems provides a runway for the development and launch of new strategies. A closely integrated organization works quickly from a unified perspective and sense of purpose. And a fully integrated organization can respond to market changes without going into panic mode. Integrated organizations have regularly scheduled time for discussions and evaluations that are proactive in nature, versus super-charged, emotion-packed deadline decisions orchestrated by senior management.

And what organization doesn't find itself in a fast-paced marketplace today?

CASE STUDY:
BUILDING ORGANIZATIONAL ALIGNMENT AND COLLABORATION

I consulted with a national education company that had created a new product customized for three very specific US markets. Before launching, the company wanted to test the acceptance and adoption of its product by key industry buyers.

Unfortunately, the demographics of the three target markets had not been deeply researched, so there was uncertainty surrounding the project. On the plus side, the company had a large group of advisors and consultants ready to help with field research.

Given these parameters, we designed a program to identify target buyers, contact them for executive interviews, compile interview results in a centralized database, and prepare the data for peer-to-peer discussion and analysis.

Because this organization was fully aligned on its core mission and values, we were able to accomplish our research touch points across the country in record time. This allowed us to spend our time analyzing the data and constructing strategic recommendations. Our work would have taken much longer if the organization had not been fully aligned and accustomed to collaboration at the outset.

Integration gives an organization the ability to address challenges by quickly creating problem-solving collaborative teams. Once a problem has been addressed, a team can disband without interruption in the overall organizational flow. When multiple problems occur simultaneously, multiple teams can be formed, which is only possible in an integrated organization. Speed and flexibility are the hallmarks of organizational integration.

In highly volatile industries, where pricing and products change rapidly, integration is essential. Yet within industries that are historically stable and predictable, organizations without integration are still vulnerable to market shifts.

In our client work, we repeatedly find that organizational integration produces motivated employees during times of market stability as well as tumultuous change. The most highly integrated organizations are also the most proactive when changes occur in their marketplace.

These are the four essential disciplines that characterize highly integrated organizations:

Discipline 1: DRIVING PRODUCT
DEVELOPMENT
Discipline 2: INSTALLING TOTAL QUALITY
MANAGEMENT
Discipline 3: BUILDING UNIFIED SALES
Discipline 4: CREATING BRAND MARKETING

While these disciplines are not unique in their merit, what makes them powerful is when they are all fully integrated throughout an organization. Together, they empower quick responses to a full range of new market conditions. Whether you're building a startup from scratch or managing a top-performing multi-national, implementing full integration will help you meet the challenges of today's competitive marketplace.

Building an organization's integration rarely comes from leadership that uses a command-and-control methodology. Just as team members prefer to be coached rather than bossed, they also look for opportunities to participate in leadership decisions. Because middle and lower team members are on the front line of communications every day, they often have insights they are able to share with their senior leaders, if they're listening.

Smart leaders seek meaningful conversations with staff at all levels. Organizational integration encourages those moments, regularly including team members in planning discussions.

This process also requires a balanced assessment of what's going on inside and outside the organization. It requires listening and responding. Done right, it can lead to a deeper understanding of the organization and how to best serve its market.

Discipline 1: DRIVING PRODUCT DEVELOPMENT

New products can transform a market when they provide an innovative solution to problems. In order for this to occur, product-development timelines must be kept short. Only an integrated organization can produce an innovation that abruptly changes a market.

Consider Uber. For decades, if you wanted to be driven from one location to another you called a taxi or a private car service. Those were your only options (unless you wanted to call a friend or drive your own car). Almost from the moment it launched, Uber changed the game by offering customers a tech option: With a few clicks on an app on your phone or tablet, an independent driver would arrive to deliver you to your destination — often at a reduced cost compared to a cab or car service.

And like any product or service that efficiently fills a market need, Uber took off, posting astronomical growth numbers year after year.

A key to product development is designing a team with representatives from various departments, including sales, marketing, research, finance, and customer service. Another is to use a "staging process" to detect and correct problems in new products prior to shipment. This simple process helps identify opportunities for continuous improvement throughout all of the organization's product development stages, and make substantial contributions to the financial bottom line. A product development process of this type can also guide an organization smoothly into ways to more fully analyze and address customer needs. This, in turn, allows an organization to chart and review customer and market-driven data for trends that can lead to further product innovation.

Integrating innovative product development into an organization's culture encourages a "We do not build defects" mindset. Systems can be put in place that can be updated by team members — not just senior leaders. And that, of course, encourages participation. Fully engaged employees will want to monitor processes that ensure new products are all they claim to be. It's a win-win.

An organization driven by integrated product development will always be looking for ways to streamline. Many turn to web-based solutions to speed up processes such as competition forecasting, cost quotations, transmitting order information to suppliers, customer queries and more.

For most innovation-driven organizations, sales from new products represent at least 20% of annual revenue. This is why new product development should be an integral part of an organization's strategy, and why updating existing products should be part of an ongoing strategy. A detailed product-to-market policy should be developed, including a quality assurance program guided by team members — without the need for direct senior leadership participation.

Over time, this essential discipline of product development will create industry recognition for innovative products and services brought to market in a timely fashion. Organizations that achieve the highest levels of product and service quality through certifications such as ISO-9001, can institutionalize continuous quality improvement as "the way we do business." Many industry leaders have installed an information-management system that provides instant access to market and product performance data, thus eliminating bottlenecks and improving product development decisions.

CASE STUDY:
INDUSTRIAL COMPANY IN TRANSITION

I consulted with a mid-market industrial company that had been in business for decades. Their product line was extensive. Yet over time, they'd lost market share to competitors, and revenues had declined.

We conducted our Organizational 360° to produce a formal market study, with customer interviews to gain further insights and perspectives. Our research showed that the company was operating in steep departmental silos, making them oblivious to market changes.

The company was currently marketing 185 products, yet 85% of total revenue came from just 15 products. Unsurprisingly, they had unsold inventory that was more than a decade old.

Clearly, their product line needed a major overhaul. We offered four recommendations: 1) Discontinue a stunning 100 products (that represented less than 10% of the annual revenues); 2) Sell all inventory that had been in the warehouse for five years or more (this brought in nearly a million dollars); 3) Refocus sales and marketing on the top 15 products; and 4) Invest in new-product development. These recommendations led to a balanced and sustainable product line that fueled the company's growth.

Discipline 2: INSTALLING TOTAL QUALITY MANAGEMENT

If you think the integration of Total Quality Management (TQM) isn't essential, think again. As *We Are Social*, the popular online media website, recently reported the number of internet users has grown enormously. Consider these statistics as of 2018:

- TOTAL WORLD POPULATION: 7.593 BILLION
- INTERNET USERS: 4.021 BILLION
- ACTIVE SOCIAL MEDIA USERS: 3.196 BILLION
- UNIQUE MOBILE USERS: 5.135 BILLION
- ACTIVE MOBILE SOCIAL USERS: 2.958 BILLION

Take-away for all organizations

If you don't focus on Total Quality Management, word of your shortcomings can spread like wildfire online. With that in mind, we've developed several dynamics to maximize TQM.

The first dynamic is prioritizing focused financial management as a top priority. The importance of a Return On Investment (ROI) cannot be overstated. Keep your eyes on the products or services that boost the bottom line, and allocate funding for innovation. The primary driver for a healthy ROI is creative breakthrough ideas.

The second dynamic is bringing customers' perspectives into your decision-making process. "Are we meeting the needs of our key customers?" is a question that should be asked frequently. And, "Where are we falling short of their expectations?" While some successful organizations prefer to stay out of the limelight and fly under the radar, you can be sure that they are all fine-tuned to their customers' opinions and needs.

The third dynamic is creating and maintaining a well-documented quality assurance program that tracks market trends and product effectiveness. This will provide cycles of continuous improvement and help identify constraining processes. TQM should be approached without fear of time, and with patience and thoroughness. Put in the time needed to ensure quality and innovation, and you'll receive dividends for years to come. Organizations that evaluate their offerings and compare them to their competitors' have much more success than those that rely upon the senior leader's next "big idea" — rarely a sustainable or scalable approach.

Does this mean there's no room for genius at the top? Absolutely not! But for every Steve Jobs and Bill Gates there are countless others who have launched untested products that went exactly nowhere. Successful organizations, with TQM fully integrated throughout, use information management to leverage primary products and services, while actively researching innovations for the future to ride the next wave of growth.

Discipline 3: BUILDING UNIFIED SALES

One of the best ways to evaluate your sales program is to analyze it alongside your marketing program. Is Marketing providing Sales with the information it needs to generate prospects? Is Sales providing Marketing with the feedback it needs to make informed judgments on strategic positioning?

Are they in continuous contact — or rarely in touch? In today's competitive world of niche markets, sales and marketing must work hand in glove.

Years ago, organizations could get by relying on independently managed sales and marketing departments, but two new market factors have changed all that: extended buying cycles, and reduced resources. As well, the old-fashioned phenomenon of "cold calling" produces limited results now. Surveys of entrepreneurial companies confirm the ineffectiveness of this approach in gaining new business.

If you think about how your sales and marketing teams were put together, you might find it was done piece-meal — despite their need for one another. It's a prescription for failure, and the reason sales and marketing programs often under-produce. Here are six practical steps to develop a unified sales strategy:

1. Market Research
- Identify top market targets.
- Create a value proposition that is more compelling than your competition's.

2. Sales & Marketing Strategy
- Align your target-market buying cycle with your organization's key objectives.
- Identify elements inside and outside of your organization to leverage resources.

3. Marketing Execution
- Create new tactics and tools to achieve your clients' goals.
- Create messaging that highlights what's new and different.

4. Lead Generation
- Inbound and outbound — understand how to grow opportunities.
- Create open communication channels between marketing and sales teams.

5. Sales Management
- Fund and maximize your top sales channels.

6. Results Analysis
- Close the loop — keep customers coming back.

CASE STUDY:
INTERNATIONAL PUBLISHER MOVES FROM PRINT TO DIGITAL PUBLISHING

A publishing house with international sales wanted a comprehensive rebranding. It had good circulation numbers among well-educated monthly subscribers to its print magazine. It also had an effective sales marketing platform that attracted new subscribers while retaining current ones in the specialty market it served.

But the company hadn't conducted formal research for many years, and was largely unaware of the demographics of its readership. Given the unusual nature of this market, we decided to conduct both quantitative research to gather demographics information regarding their target market, and qualitative research to learn first-hand of their customers' needs.

Once the data was gathered and analyzed we concluded that a digital edition could be successfully promoted to current readers, and would be welcomed by a new and younger audience as well. The publisher designed a digital magazine and began marketing it to both current and prospective subscribers. Current customers added the digital offering while retaining the print edition, while the younger prospects subscribed to the digital offering alone. After three years, the publisher's worldwide circulation grew from 600,000 subscriptions to more than one million.

Integration plays an important role in creating a unified sales program because it connects the organization's sales promises to its marketing strategy. Creating and maintaining such a program ensures that the strategy is fully integrated throughout the organization and its market.

Discipline 4: CREATING BRAND MARKETING

Brand marketing has never been more important. To answer clients' needs I designed a four-step process, called The Four P's of Branding, that can be used either to create a new brand or fix an existing one. As illustrated below, The Four P's are Purpose, Promise, Personality and Platform.

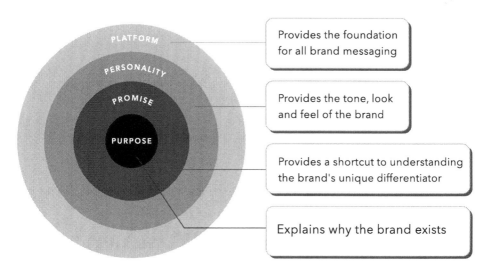

PLATFORM
PERSONALITY
PROMISE
PURPOSE

Provides the foundation for all brand messaging

Provides the tone, look and feel of the brand

Provides a shortcut to understanding the brand's unique differentiator

Explains why the brand exists

MarketCues 4 P's of Branding™

Senior leaders can use these four brand P's to identify gaps between their own perception and what the marketplace thinks.

Purpose: What is the true purpose of our brand? What an organization says and does should always be the same — that's obvious. Less obvious is the need to deliver a unique product or service. If this question can't be easily answered, no marketing campaign in the world can help the brand.

Promise: What brand promises do we make? It's best to define one to three promises that represent a brand's purpose. If, for example, your brand is a mobile app that promises "Highest Mobile Security," make sure that's a tried-and-true fact.

Personality: What is the personality of our brand? Take a look at the way your employees behave and sound; that has a lot to do with your customers' experiences with your brand. A positive interaction between a customer and a representative of your organization establishes a positive brand image (and the opposite is true as well).

Platform: What is the platform of our brand? To answer this question you need to research the social and business media platforms your prospective customers use. Linear social-media programs, although very busy, typically fail.

Using the Four P's illustration:

- When designing a new brand, begin with the brand's Purpose, then move to Promise, and continue outward.

- When fixing an existing brand, begin with the outer ring, Platform, to determine your effectiveness on all media platforms. Correct problems, if they exist, then move to Personality, and continue inward.

CASE STUDY:
HOW INNOVATION CHANGED AN INDUSTRY

A large manufacturing company entered a well-established market as the new kid on the block. With worldwide sales larger than the top leader in the US, its total US revenues were modest. But they had something that their chief competitor lacked: Innovation. In fact, this manufacturer had developed a product that held the potential to revolutionize the industry.

Given this unique situation, we recommended our client put the majority of its branding budget into a one-product campaign that would saturate the market with news of its revolutionary innovation. This was a risky approach: What if the innovation tanked? Would it erode their existing products?

We designed a re-purchase program in which the manufacturer would buy back a competitor's products held by the customer, install its new equipment at no charge, and provide product service support for five years. The only thing a customer had to do was guarantee that all consumables for this new equipment would be purchased from our client for a like period of five years.

The approach paid off. The manufacturer's innovation went from zero sales to the top-seller in its market category, leading to substantial increased revenue for years to come.

When strategizing a brand launch, keep in mind:

Visual — How does it look?

Today's market sectors are filled with well-designed materials and presentations. You want your brand to be at or above the aesthetic level of the competition. New ideas and concepts require powerful visuals. For a new product, you might consider an interactive website video. Videos can be as short or long as necessary, as long as you make every moment count.

Emotional — How does it make me feel?

If your organization is known for using facts and formulas in an analytical bottom-line approach, your brand marketing should have a similarly analytical feel. On the other hand, a product or service for the entertainment industry needs to convey creativity. Wherever your organization is on that spectrum, your target audience needs to believe that you know what you're talking about by the choices you've made in branding.

Functional — How does it work?

In the business marketplace, a common branding mistake is to point everything to just one type of person or position responsible for purchases — a CEO or CFO type. In fact, a brand campaign with broader-based appeal is more effective.

Financial — How is it priced?

Pricing is the least scientific of all the elements. Obviously you want your price to be competitive, but the market can be unpredictable. Apple's success proved that high-price products can dominate a market if consumers feel they're worth it. Still, you need to do your due diligence: How do other executives in your industry solve problems and select products? The more you know about your competitors, the better you are able to position and compose a successful brand campaign.

Target Market Profile

Transactional: Logical decision-making coupled with high integrity standards.

Emotional: High-energy and makes decisions on how things look and sound.

Relational: Driven by personality and relationships.

Functional: Concerned about qualitative thinking and processes.

If your targeted customers tend to be Transactional, you need a strong ROI value proposition. If they tend to be Emotional, you need a highly inspirational value proposition. Relational executives tend to make decisions based on assessments of others' talents. Functional executives base decisions on hard data — facts and figures.

Some brands will never get a foothold in a market filled with fierce competition. Other brands, with dwindling sales, should be put out to pasture, having outgrown their relevance.

How many mission statements look good on paper but have little to do with products and services brought to the marketplace? Using online platforms, customers are more informed than ever before — including how well your brand delivers on its promises. Claims like "Highest quality" and "Excellent service" are meaningless if the court of public opinion — on Facebook, Yelp and dozens of other sites — rules otherwise.

Smart executives at all levels understand the importance of driving strategic growth. And most senior executives know that brand strategy is important to their organization's success. But when it comes to the hard work of building an effective branding program, implementing key strategies and sustainability programs, many need guidance and encouragement.

Three Ways To Brand Like A Pro

Begin with a brand review, or in marketer's parlance, a brand audit. This is the most efficient way to unify style, tone, messaging, and other communications. It will reveal a brand's true market valuation, as well as gaps that have been overlooked, and mistakes that need to be corrected.

Although big data is a wonderful tool, the brand review process should not be automated. Human insights and judgments will pay big dividends here. Using data as a basis for their assessments, audit reviewers need to remember:

1) Keep it Distinctive

It's always a temptation to be all things to all people, but nothing weakens a brand like a watered-down, please-the-crowd approach.

2) Keep it Interactive

Regardless of the size of the company you're leading, you probably have a lot of stories like your company's history and information to share with new customers. Find an interactive way to engage in a dialogue with them.

3) Keep it Simple

Beware the clever or trendy theme: When it goes out of style, so does your brand. The best approach matches your brand's unique qualities with a unique presentation. Easier said than done — but worth the effort.

To stay current and relevant, make brand reviews an ongoing practice. It should not be something you have to do, but something you want to do. That's thinking like a pro. No one sets out to damage their strategic marketing. But sometimes it happens.

Let's take a look at three common mistakes you'll want to avoid. The first is expecting too much of your audience. People are hit with hundreds if not thousands of marketing messages every day. We'd all go nuts if we paid attention to more than a tiny fraction of them. So your first baby steps — if your company or organization is not already well known — is simply to build a connection to your target market. And be patient. You will build trust and gain ground with your honesty and integrity and follow-through.

The second mistake is expecting too much from your own company. Again, if you're not well known, you won't get instant results. One good way to start a conversation about your brand is to begin with an issue or topic that already interests your audience. Maybe you're aware of a problem being discussed on social media, and you can address it — maybe even offer a solution.

Finally, you may expect too much from your marketing campaign. It doesn't have to be terrible to be ignored. There's bound to be some trial and error. What's important is that you deliver on all the promises you make for your products — and keep trying. If you are realistic about your company's current position in the market, and plan strategic marketing accordingly, with time you'll find an approach that resonates with your audience.

Chapter Summary

Organizational integration provides a clear definition of goals, values and operations that are aligned throughout the organization. This gives leaders and team members the ability to make informed decisions at critical junctures. It's particularly important at times when a new strategy, with budget and timeline parameters, is being implemented. Issues that can eat up dozens of planning sessions will be managed in a fraction of the time by a fully integrated organization. That's because:

• Leaders and team members have agreed which products will be developed and which will be discontinued.

• Leaders have clearly communicated how their Total Quality Management program is going to be implemented and have put in place safeguards for a high standard of excellence.

• Leaders and team members have taken the necessary steps to unify its sales and marketing programs, and have placed a strong emphasis on delivering on brand promises.

• Leaders and team members have created brand marketing that truly represents the organization's strategy and culture, and have found an effective way to communicate them to the marketplace.

During the next chapter, RETHINK Your Organization's Awareness, we will explore how successful leaders leverage their organization's integrated goals, values and operations to drive high awareness inside and outside their organization.

Driver 3:
RETHINK YOUR ORGANIZATION'S AWARENESS

ORGANIZATIONAL awareness means that all employees understand the organization's operations, culture, mission and values and anything else that defines it. Once an organization has a strong alignment and deep integration of purpose at full throttle, it can confidently drive awareness to create a clear path to success.

This requires leaders and team members to say what they mean and do what they say. This fuels and drives the organization's awareness. In fact, nothing builds momentum faster.

Organizations that implement a strategic plan that is aligned to its goals and integrates them throughout the organization are 12% more profitable than those that don't, according to Mission Facilitators International (MFI). Astoundingly, MFI also reports that 95% of the typical workforce doesn't understand or even know their organization's strategy. We've found two reason this is the case: 1) Organizations rarely link strategy to budget; and 2) Most executive teams spend less than an hour a month discussing strategy. Given these two factors, it's easy to understand why an organization's awareness would be low.

It's ironic that although organizations of all types and sizes use these concepts every day, there is a gross misunderstanding of how they work. The majority of leaders and their teams agree they could greatly increase their organization's awareness, but knowing how to unravel this traffic jam remains a mystery to many.

Part of the problem of building awareness is due to its degree of complexity. It requires a cohesive understanding of the organization's many interrelated dimensions, including its operations, organizational structure, culture and associated behaviors. And these are further impacted by external factors such as economic, social and political issues.

In order for an organization to build awareness, all of these factors need to be understood. This requires a level of understanding that goes beyond simply doing daily routines and tasks. It means that everyone has a deep knowledge of the organization's strategic positioning and knows how to deliver it.

Another benefit of awareness is hiring new employees is easier and increases employee retention. Employees place a high value on organizations that possess great purpose and provide opportunities to contribute. When employees understand and believe in their organization's mission — what it stands for and why it's important — they respond in positive proactive ways that add value, and this drives awareness.

When we rethink an organization's awareness we research how they perceive their strengths and weaknesses. We then compare these perceptions to those held by those they serve. Often the differences between them are dramatic.

During multiple consulting engagements, I have observed senior leaders often think their organization's awareness is low because of deficiencies with team members. Yet I have found in many instances, this is simply not true. Often it is due to a general confusion about how to drive awareness throughout the organization and its market. This causes conflict.

The most difficult situation occurs when team members understand this awareness challenge, but their senior leader doesn't. This blind spot at the top risks an organization's health and growth, and even its survival. This is because the culture of an organization is a reflection of itself. Positive cultures create positive awareness. So if an organization's culture is negative it will thwart the organization's ability to create positive awareness.

You might be thinking, oh come on, organizations take the time to figure out how to increase their awareness! However, a quick look at the long list of failed businesses suggests otherwise. In fact, business analysts constantly identify underperforming organizations. Consider these statistics: Only one out of ten organizations will make it to year 10, and of those that do, only one of those 10 will make it to year 20. Clearly there is a gap between the energy put into *starting* an organization versus *building* one and staying in business.

We have found this particularly true of organizations going through an organizational transformation. There are several tips we offer to clients that are going through a change. They are relevant no matter the size or type of organization:

- Keep the "Big Picture" in mind and address issues that can be solved quickly within its context.

- Accept criticism gracefully—knowing it will surely come.

- Avoid a "One and Done Syndrome"

perspective that focuses on a single detail.

- Provide leadership opportunities for everyone, not just those with big titles.

- Take enough time to ensure you have all of the facts before you begin making changes.

There are two major influencers that drive awareness:

Influencer 1: Business Model Management — internal to the organization

Influencer 2: Marketplace Development — external to the organization

When the two influencers operate in concert they create healthy, positive awareness within the organization and its marketplace.

Influencer 1: BUSINESS MODEL MANAGEMENT

A business model defines the logic that drives how an organization creates and delivers its value to those it serves. It's a roadmap of how to move the organization through its economic, social and cultural decisions. It provides a consistent basis to form and judge decisions. It's a way to quickly know what the organization will and won't do based upon a predetermined set of values and beliefs. When the organization's business model is understood by both leaders and team members, everyone is able to quantify a wide range of proposals and "feel" if they are on track.

Embedded into a business model is a value proposition that succinctly states the promise of value the organization will deliver. This clear definition informs employees as well as customers what they can count on from the organization.

Leaders who are unable to quickly state in a single sentence their organization's value proposition usually experience organizational challenges. This is because if they cannot easily explain how they can solve their employees' and customers' challenges they will have a difficult time leading their team.

For example, Starbucks Coffee's value proposition, from the company's inception, was that their stores would become every customer's second family room. This concept was simple and easy to understand. The design of their stores makes conversations over coffee, tea, and meals easy and comfortable. They're not trying to be a restaurant or even a coffee shop! They are a high-quality place to hold a meeting or get together with friends. Their food and drink products are simply how they make money. The place is how they attract people to their stores. Their wild success is also attributable to the design of the stores themselves. Its value proposition propelled a single coffeehouse in Seattle to become a global corporation with nearly 30,000 outlets.

Employees place a high value on organizations that possess great purpose and provide opportunities to contribute. When employees understand and believe in their organization's mission — what it stands for and why it's important — they respond in positive proactive ways that add value, and this drives awareness.

Business models should also be designed with the organization's values to help guide everyone to do the "right thing." Core values might include one or more of the following:

- Integrity
- Honesty
- Quality
- Healthy
- Dependability
- Reliability
- Loyalty
- Accountability

A succinct understanding of the organization's values embedded into the business model drives awareness throughout the organization. Absent are questions about "Who are we?" and "What is our primary purpose for being here?" This clarity builds positive awareness inside the organization. It really is that simple.

A Formal Business Model Is Scalable

A business model creates sustainable and scalable awareness for the organization that fulfills the needs of those it serves. It places a demand on both leaders and team members to take deliberate steps that deliver its promises. Once in place, it enables all employees to self-judge their own performances, and that improves the organization as a whole.

An effective business model asks five questions that drive awareness:

1. Have we identified our target market and planned how we are going to reach potential customers?
2. Are we able to consistently provide offerings our customers most want?
3. Will we meet or exceed our daily performance expectations at every level of our organization?
4. Are our offerings so well differentiated that none of our competitors are able to duplicate them?
5. What are the key factors that will ensure we maintain profitability?

How a Business Model Drives Awareness

A formal business model can be developed for two scenarios: Short-term (1-year) and Long-term (3-5 years), with semi-annual organizational reviews.

This allows the organization to drive department-specific strategies from a single business model. By transitioning from various independent programs to one organizational strategy, the organization can more easily communicate with its market. This shift is simple for everyone in the organization to understand. It holds great power. It lifts the organization and makes it easy to communicate with its market. When this occurs, it raises awareness.

As an organization grows it can move into multiple markets. Strategic decisions concerning which markets to pursue should be made within the context of a formal business model. Organizations that leverage their business model don't need to use a traditional "Features and Benefits" approach to build market awareness. One serious strategic mistake I have observed is when organizations form their decisions based upon what has worked in the past or what is working for one of their competitors. This is a mistake an organization will likely regret.

CASE STUDY:
PROFESSIONAL SERVICES CORPORATION WITH HIGH OVERHEAD AND LOW PROFITABILITY

During a consulting engagement I identified a family member on the executive team who brought little value to the business, yet his salary was in the mid six figures. It was easy for me to see that this family member was not producing close to his expected ROI and yet he remained highly compensated. Unsurprisingly, this blatant nepotism – the man was the CEO's brother – had created resentment among non-family team members and had led to the loss of a number of the top producers. Talk about a difficult situation.

After the CEO and I had a number of frank discussions, he confronted his brother in a professional way, even though it was uncomfortable, letting him know what would be expected of him going forward. This calm approach left open room for him to change. After six months the family member left the company to pursue alternative opportunities.

Almost immediately the company's morale improved and produced many positive employee efforts that drove awareness inside and outside the company. And using the brother's inflated salary, the CEO was able to attract new producers, who boosted sales to rise again to its previous years.

To achieve high awareness there may be times you will have to meet your challenges head on – even if it's a bit painful for the moment. This CEO learned that his challenges were really opportunities hiding in plain sight. The lack of positive awareness throughout the organization had dragged the company down. With one decisive move, the CEO corrected the situation. It just took courage.

Influencer 2: MARKETPLACE DEVELOPMENT

Marketplace development is built on a growth strategy that seeks new market opportunities. It leverages the organization's business model by emphasizing its embedded values and promises. This allows the organization to service an existing market and build a new one to expand its reach and growth.

Every organization needs to understand what current and prospective customers want. This knowledge fuels market development as the organization learns more and improves its position, which in turn drives the awareness of the organization. For smaller firms with limited budgets, gaining market knowledge can be challenging. And even the strongest organizations can face challenges during major market swings that catch them off guard.

This is why all organizations — large and small — need to budget for ongoing market development and not solely rely on their present knowledge. To attract new customers, you have to know their specific needs and how to meet them. Leaders who say their team just needs to "keep their eyes and ears open" are usually the ones caught off guard during market swings. And all markets swing.

Many companies do not differentiate among corporate, product and brand strategies. As long as sales are rising, this type of developmental analysis doesn't seem necessary. Frankly, that approach can have dire consequences that are difficult to avoid.

Think of a brand that once occupied a leadership position but no longer does. Now ask yourself, "What went wrong?" The answer will be one or more of the following:

- Their corporate image became associated with an "old fashioned" technology position.

- Their product no longer met the needs of its customers, but they kept on pushing the product into the marketplace where it was ultimately labeled irrelevant.

- They were part of a disastrous merger. Why disastrous? Because the two companies' cultures were totally different, their management styles didn't match up — hence they couldn't make strategic decisions.

Being decisive through this planning process will help the organization grow when you listen carefully to all inputs and engage in a healthy debate with your team. Once all of the voices have been heard and you've taken time to design the type of culture you'd prefer, it's time for everyone to get behind it and pursue the organization's goals. It is extremely helpful for both leaders and staff to fully understand what the guiding cultural beliefs and values will be to guide their decisions using a solid context.

The best place to start when developing a business market is to gather competitive analysis from industry leaders. It takes some effort to seek them out and gain their interest in sharing what's happening in their industry. But most of the time when two-way information sharing is promised, leaders become willing to share their insights with those it perceives are in earnest of their perspectives. This newly gained market intelligence can be leveraged to drive development and campaigns, to expand an organization's portfolio of offerings and to increase its market share.

When an organization's market is fully developed it has tied its business model to its competitive analysis. This fuels the organization's top priorities and drives effective awareness.

CASE STUDY:
NATIONAL BUSINESS FOUND NEW MARKET TRACTION BY INCREASING ITS AWARENESS

I consulted with 11 State and Federal Agencies on how they could gain a significant boost in their market position. They had been operating for years within a public private cooperative and had grown to a significant size. However, the organization had not been able to learn how to work together with an effective collaboration. Collectively, their market intelligence was substantial, but due to their organizational dysfunction each agency kept its specific market data to itself.

What was required was a major transformation of strategic direction in order to unravel their dysfunction and create a winning solution. Using our Organizational 360°, we benchmarked 3,500 online assessments and conducted 35 executive-level interviews. This allowed us to aggregate the attitudes, knowledge and perceptions into a cohesive database. With this in hand, we tested the organizations' awareness by conducting public forums involving customers, industry leaders and the business media.

All of our gathered research pointed toward the need for one strategic growth plan to drive awareness of the agencies' collaboration, versus their specific agencies. So we presented our findings and plan to the 11 agency chiefs.

To gain each of the agencies' buy-in, tangible benefits were presented to convince them of the value of collaboration. The primary benefits would be an increase in customers, and profitability while at the same time reducing the cost of marketing. This approach provided a collective of market intelligence they individually lacked. Our plan was accepted, and quickly funneled the agencies' divergent perspectives and insights into an effective awareness program. The CEO of the collective reported that the program provided the critical business information needed for a double-digit awareness increase.

The Danger of the "Not Invented Here Syndrome"

The 'Not Invented Here Syndrome' (NIHS) is a slightly tongue-in-cheek name for the tendency of leaders and even entire organizations to reject suitable external solutions to internal problems in favor of internally developed solutions. Often found in large corporations, this mindset is prevalent within organizations that do not benchmark any of its external best practices. They believe their inventions and offerings are superior to their competitions' and on that basis rule out researching anything else. During my years of executive organizational consulting I have observed those who prefer to insulate themselves using only internal resources often experience overwhelming competitive challenges. And I've found that these organizations rarely have data to substantiate the claims that often lead to their decline.

Healthy and growing organizations, or ones that want to grow, can build their market knowledge by gathering all types of market data. Using external service providers increases the organization's understanding of the markets it serves and how to grow their organization.

The three reasons leaders most commonly state for not wanting to use outside service providers are:

1.   It will take too much time.
2.   It will cost too much.
3.   It will disrupt my organization.

To be fair, for some organizations — at certain points in their development — one or all of these reasons may be true. But here's the irony: This is typically when the organization requires the most outside help! Yet, the NIHS left unchecked will allow this defective management practice to remain.

Marketplace development includes benchmarking customer needs and designing ways to meet them. Even using an informal benchmarking mechanism within a market can help an organization strengthen its offerings.

Team members with relationships in targeted external markets should be encouraged to bring in new ideas and suggestions. Leaders may be surprised by what team members already know and can quickly contribute. To encourage this kind of dialogue, try asking:

- Have we benchmarked competitive data to drive innovation that is helping us become a market leader?

- Do we gather customer input with current competitive analysis to create a stronger market position?

- Have we formalized competitive information and cross-indexed it to our products and services?

- Do we have leading indicator metrics to monitor our competition?

- Have we conducted scenario-planning sessions with leadership and their team members to determine optimal outcomes most desired by the organization?

- Have we identified "Hot Buttons" that can be used to effectively present our offerings to build our marketplace?

The new marketplace

As I have said several times before, the internet has changed the world. Given the continuous marketplace changes, organizations need a strong market development program that can make changes quickly. There are early warning signs that can alert leaders when changes are needed. But the senior leader needs to see the challenges and have the courage to implement change. The leader's willingness to see reality is the single most important ingredient for building organizational change and awareness. A leader that understands what's really going on can find solutions that solve his or her organization's toughest challenges.

Challenges that signal immediate change is required:
- Monthly sales decline
- High employee attrition
- Negative customer feedback
- Strategy meetings that don't lead to decisions.

Building a high market awareness does not require a senior leader with a charismatic personality. But he or she does need a strong business knowledge based on an equally strong market knowledge that will meet customers' needs. If you are the senior leader of an organization, you know how important your leadership team is to its success. This is not only critical for sustaining the organization but also for growing its awareness.

As CEO you need to know:
1. Your organization's greatest strength is its

internal talent on staff, not its external products and services.

2. Your organization's greatest challenges are internal, not external.
3. Your organization's success will be judged by your customers, not you.

Anyone involved in building the awareness for their organization can benefit from AIDA, an acronym for Attention, Interest, Desire and Action. AIDA is one of the founding models for modern-day marketing and awareness building. In fact, we have found that if your awareness campaign is missing just one of the four AIDA steps, it will fail. AIDA is simple to use:

- Attention – get customers' attention: surprise them.
- Interest – hold their attention: listen to customers' challenges; you ask the questions and let them do the talking and then help find the solutions.
- Desire – demonstrate how your products are uniquely suited to solving their challenges.
- Action – ask customers to take the next step. But be careful here. Don't push something the market isn't ready for. Maybe the next stage is more information, or a product demo. The key is to keep the ball rolling in the direction you want it to go.

AIDA builds great value and awareness for an organization. Just 10 years ago most sales presentations were made in person but that has dramatically changed in the digital marketplace, where virtual meetings are the norm. Motivating potential customers through the various AIDA stages will lead to the kinds of personal relationships that are so important to building awareness.

CASE STUDY:
LEADING UNIVERSITY INSTITUTE DISCOVERED NEW WAYS TO DRIVE ITS AWARENESS

I was asked to consult with a university institute that offered graduate programs for continuing education. The institute had moved into a major period of change and recognized the need for a full transformation. This engagement included a deep dive into their organizational design and an analysis of key markets. Specific knowledge areas were selected that could be benchmarked to identify any profound gaps of perception between the institute and its students.

We found that many departments were operating as islands to themselves, without shared awareness among them. As a result, they'd created a siloed organization over many years and had lost touch with how students perceived the institute. This negatively impacted the university's ability to gain valuable feedback from its students and gain their buy-in for new programs and policies. Not surprisingly, this organizational dysfunction had stalled the university institute's health and growth.

Following our review, we recommended the institute implement a Circular Organizational Structure to flatten it and to allow leaders and team members to collaborate more easily and productively. Major updates to existing programs were identified along with several new online Master's Level Programs.

A five-year adaptive plan with monthly KPI-driven dashboard metrics provided the institute's leadership with continuous feedback concerning what was working well and what needed further development. Within one year the institute had substantially improved its market perception and awareness while also operating with a more effective management system. This improved its ability to manage departments as one team versus the silos that had been in operation. And, by combining the marketing and sales departments into one department, a unified customer awareness program was achieved.

Building organizational awareness requires a rigorous, nimble analytical process for valuing a market's potential and mining new opportunities. All organizations have a measurable amount of credibility in its defined markets. So it's important to leverage this credibility in positive ways by maximizing opportunities that strengthen the organization's strategic positioning. In addition, routinely reviewing these critical decisions will keep the organization on track with what customers most want.

Organizations with high market awareness use a formal assessment tool to review the progress of its primary products and services, based upon their performance. This performance is then measured against an organization's strategy plan. This creates a proactive culture that encourages continuous improvement. Leaders who don't understand the importance of incremental assessments and improvement often think of anything but total success as a failure. Nothing could be further from the truth.

Each experience should be thought of as a learning opportunity that encourages continuous improvement. Leadership teams operating with this continuous improvement strategy outperform those driven by micro-management. Micro-managed employees feel under-powered and even helpless in the decision making process, so their motivation trends downward.

When employees enjoy a truly open and positive atmosphere, this motivates them to participate and tell others about their organization. This grows awareness inside and outside the organization and eliminates the need for lengthy meetings. A welcome change for anyone who has had to endure them.

The organization that uses analytical tools to gain market and cultural intelligence will improve its products and services. Organizations that understand how to best work within this positive and collaborative framework will make better decisions. Smart organizations do not base decisions solely on one set of criteria or level of leadership. Rather, they take into account all internal and external input, including assessments of their competitors. When there is a formal mechanism for benchmarking other organizations within their marketplace, this added understanding greatly assists the organization in developing its strategies.

An organization's awareness can more quickly become negative if its leadership team does not proactively encourage positive teamwork. Nothing creates positive organizational awareness faster and better than one that is motivated to meet the needs of its customers and has created metrics that are designed to monitor and improve its abilities compared to its competitors.

Chapter Summary

Organizational awareness requires many moving parts working together in one steady stream throughout all phases of the organization. Awareness begins with a rock-solid understanding of the organization's alignment — its vision, mission, and values — and every effort has been made to integrate this understanding throughout the organization. A fully integrated organization will have mastered the two key Influencers of the Awareness Driver: Business Model Management and Marketplace Development. And it will be able to confirm the following:

- Our organization uses a strategic plan that is aligned to our goals and has integrated them with employees and customers.
- Our organization understands its many interrelated dimensions, including its operations, organizational structure, culture and how it should behave in the marketplace.
- Our organization conducts scenario-planning sessions with leadership and their team members to determine the outcomes most desired by the organization.
- Our organization synthesizes customer input with current competitive analysis to create a strong market position.
- Our organization benchmarks competitive data to drive an organization-wide innovation.

Driver 4:

RETHINK YOUR ORGANIZATION'S RELEVANCE

THE fourth driver for building a healthy and growing organization is relevance. This is the final step after an organization has been aligned, integrated on all levels, and its awareness is well-known in-house and in the marketplace. When those three drivers are functioning at a high level, then it's time to address and build relevance.

Relevance in today's uncertain business climate is key to the only true job security. Change has become the norm, job security is the exception. These tumultuous changes impact everyone, particularly the business community, where change has become the new new.

But this does not mean that there is no hope. Far from it. Some organizations have figured out the way to remain safe and secure. Their secret? They've figured out how to be relevant.

Merriam-Webster's defines "relevance" as "the state of being closely connected or appropriate to the matter at hand." For an organization to be relevant, an action or person must be connected to a larger plan, a big idea that leads to the matter at hand. This requires an organization to constantly prove its relevance by making it an integral part of its standard operations. It means being the type of organization that employees and customers can depend on for excellent leadership, timely product innovations, content expertise and meaningful support. It means being authentic and trustworthy, and responsive to marketplace ebbs and flows.

Put in other words, relevant organizations' customers don't worry about product defects and employees don't worry about being mistreated on the job. This is because relevant organizations always operate with a singularity of purpose and excellence that defines who they are and what they do.

Being authentic is at the heart of relevance. Authenticity makes it easy for everyone to understand what an organization cares about, and get to know what it stands for. This is comforting because it eliminates the guesswork from relationships. This should be true for both employees and customers alike. The stronger the organization's relationships, the greater relevance it will have in its market.

Today's marketplace is fast-paced and more transparent than ever before. As a result, an organization can quickly fall out of favor in days or weeks whereas it might have taken months or years before. Strong leadership holds organizational relevance together, but this is not reserved for those at the top. Today, a highly relevant organization needs to understand — at all levels — these principles and embrace them.

Leadership must empower everyone in the organization to be a leader in their area. When this exists, an organization's true relevance will be felt and communicated. This should be a dynamic that is practiced daily. The traditional matrix structure of an organization — where a few lead at the top and everyone else follows — went out the window when the internet arrived. But many organizations do not understand that flat organizations communicate more effectively and build relevance faster.

Organizations that can make quick decisions at all levels will outpace traditional ones that need to wade through several management layers before making one. For example, in the computer chip manufacturing industry, lead times from design to launch once took two to five years. They now take two to five months. In the strategic planning area, rapid prototyping has become the preferred method to test new designs in the market versus lengthy planning scenarios. This quick paced decision making drives an organization's relevance by demonstrating its leadership.

Regardless of an organization's size, it needs to be able to leverage diverse and complimentary processes that meet its customers' demands. If an organization keeps pace with these new market realities it will find itself with high relevance leading its competition. To remain relevant, the leadership team needs to help its team members perform at the breakneck speed that is now required of all modern organizations.

Most problems within an organization stem from its misalignment and that weakens its relevance in the market. I mean no disrespect to any leader but after decades of running my own firm I know the very real challenges senior leaders face. At the end of every leader's day the question remains, "Did I help clear the way for my organization to become more relevant or did I hold it back?"

Organizations that don't adjust to these marketplace ebbs and flows will find themselves battling many challenges that are difficult to face. Organizations with rigid business processes will find it increasingly difficult to remain connected to its employees and customers. Because in this new marketplace, an organization needs to be able to quickly adapt to changing market conditions. We have found two indicators shared by relevant organizations:

Indicator 1: CUSTOMER RELATIONSHIP MANAGEMENT (CRM)

Indicator 2: CUSTOMER LOYALTY

Organizations with both of these two indicators in action always achieve the highest relevance scores because they are the best at understanding their customers' true needs and providing them with excellent solutions. They are best at building momentum in their market through word-of-mouth and good will. These indicators work together to form a stronger, sustainable and scalable organization.

Indicator 1: CUSTOMER RELATIONSHIP MANAGEMENT (CRM)

A successful CRM program begins with a clearly defined understanding of customers' needs. Everyone knows that customers should always come first and a strong connection with them is paramount. A mentor of mine in Chicago often said — "People are more important than the project. Once the project becomes more important than the people, it's time to shut down the project."

Effectively managing customer relationships

ensures strong relevance. There are four ways to build your CRM program:

1. Be Authentic

The fastest way to establish customer relationships is to embed who the organization is into everything. This full expression allows everyone to quickly communicate the organization's value. People from all types of markets and cultures are drawn to organizations that are simple to understand and powerful in what they provide.

Trying to be all things to all people is a loser's game. No organization, not even a gigantic corporation, can be all things to all people. But what they can be is a total expert in their special slice that makes them stand out: not just an expert, but the expert. Authenticity establishes an organization's customer relationships because it makes it easy for everyone to understand and trust what they're offering.

2. Be Competent

How many times have you visited a website that listed 20 or more services despite the fact they were very small? I used to notice this in the marketing industry when a firm would literally list all services in the broad categories of marketing, communications, public relations, direct mail, fundraising, sales promotion, public speaking, and the list would go on and on. These firms never established a meaningful relevance in their marketplace because they attempted to be all things to all people.

When your organization is an expert in a specific slice of the pie it becomes highly promotable and shareable because it is very easy to understand what is being offered. Arriving at this singularity of purpose requires a whittling down of programs, products, services and related offerings that the organization is going to provide; and just as importantly what the organization is not going to provide.

One quick way to accomplish this whittling down process is to ask three questions:

- What are you going to Start Doing that you're not doing now?
- What are you going to Stop Doing that you're doing now?
- What are you going to Continue Doing that you're doing now?

3. Be empathetic

The third way an organization can build its customer relationships is by actually caring about the people they serve. Empathy is one of those touchy-feely qualities that some leaders shy away from or frankly dismiss. Yet, in nearly every organization we research, we find that the top leaders in any given market are those who value empathy and are the most effective in developing and maintaining rich customer relationships.

Being empathetic is a powerful tool for building relationships within an organization and in its dealings with customers. It takes leaders and team members who have a desire to help other people in any way they can. It may require some retraining of leaders and team members who have not experienced an empathetic business environment, but it's worth the effort. Empathy will pay huge dividends to those who embrace it.

I've personally seen many instances when a team member found a solution to a customer's problem that the customer himself didn't even know he had — and bring that solution to the customer without being asked. What better way is there to prove the organization cares about them? Which leads us to the fourth way organizations can build customer relationships.

4. Be deliberate

An organization's claims for itself are one way people judge it, but the more important way it's judged is by what it actually does. Actions speak louder than words, as the old saw has it. When an organization does exactly what it claims it will do — that's proof of its relevance.

CASE STUDY:
CORPORATE COLLEGE INCREASES ITS REVENUE BY INCREASING ITS RELEVANCE

I was asked by a corporate college to consult during their strategic planning process. The client had stalled growth and they wanted to pinpoint the contributing facts. Of course, they had their own ideas but they wanted to pinpoint the specific challenges and how to solve them.

For 50 years, this college had successfully met the needs of its constituents but had fallen out of favor with its more reliable partnerships. The sheer number of training certificates they awarded each year placed them among the top-ranked corporate colleges in the US. Yet, their overall relevance had decreased due to the increase of new competitive educational institutions and specialty training firms.

Using our Organizational 360° we determined the college's true market position and the reasons for declining market relevance. Real-time data allowed us to make critical strategic judgements concerning the college's ability to sustain and scale its market image.

Many of the college's newer executive and elite management training programs were largely unknown to its key customers. This had occurred because the college had significantly curtailed its external marketing budget during a major economic development downturn. For several years this did not impact the college but as the years passed an undesirable relevance score was produced.

Unaided recall placed the college below a 50% recognition score in its primary market, the first in its long history. As a result, we recommended the college create a new marketing campaign to run for a full year based on the concept, "We did it first. We do it best." This campaign projected the college into the market's limelight and over time restored the market's knowledge of it and ultimately led to a substantial rise in its relevance score.

It's worth noting that regaining market relevance takes at least twice as long as developing it from scratch because negative perceptions are more difficult to change.

Organizations who claim to really care about their customers and have not acted on ways to prove it find themselves with weak customer relationships. What you do is far more important than what you say, and it works best when your organization actually does precisely what it says it will do.

Any frequent flyer knows that the airline industry is filled with companies that say one thing and do another. All claim to be the number one in something and yet how many times have you waited at a gate only to find your flight is cancelled because the crew timed out? Or there were equipment problems. Or, or, or.

Yes, as you may have surmised, these are all situations I have experienced that knocked down my feeling of trust toward the airline companies who promised one thing and delivered another. Your actions either move you closer to building relationships or tarnish them. An organization may be brilliant or have a brilliant product or program, but if it can't consistently deliver it will not build a positive trusting reputation — and sales will inevitably erode.

Three Practical Steps for Building Customer Relationships

Step 1: Install a centralized Customer Relationship Management (CRM) program (such as SalesForce. com or PipeDrive.com) and make it accessible to the front-line of the organization including sales and customer support teams. Once installed, it will improve organizational communications and increase relevance among customers. Creating a system for the organization to communicate and track projects, products and services will also improve its operations.

I am always amazed at how many organizations have not invested in an integrated CRM program.

Often they are siloed in various departments that compound the problem by operating several different systems that are not integrated. It's not uncommon for a company to have one program for financial, another for sales, and another for product development. This siloing makes it hard for organizations to adapt to change and get the word out about exciting new developments. And it's a major constraint on any organization trying to increase its relevance in the market.

Step 2: Make the CRM program accessible to all staff throughout the organization. This comprehensive approach will provide a channel for everyone to read and interact with customer input. That improves one-to-one communications with customers that help solve their challenges more quickly. Our research shows that when this type of program is installed it produces high relevance scores from customers who appreciate the instant access everyone has to their vital information.

Step 3: Open up a cloud-based solution that allows both the organization and its customers to input their top challenges and needs along with their suggestions on how to improve the organization's products and services. Use this information to build out each customer's current CRM profile for future sales and customer support. This requires strong management and cannot be accomplished with a light-hearted approach from leadership because people today expect quick answers to their issues. If this management support is not something your organization can commit to it is advisable to not take this third step until it is fully prepared to support it.

This cloud-based system will ensure that all sales promotion activities (including sales promotion analysis and tracking of a client's account history for repeated or future sales) are available 24/7. Ample research demonstrates that CRM programs encourage internal organization and customer behavior that is consistent with an organization's overall strategy, direction, and values. This is accomplished by systematically providing team members and customers alike with up-to-the minute information they can use to build their organization. And of course, this greatly strengthens customer relationships.

Establishing Relevance

To establish lasting relevance, an organization needs to consistently want to learn more and improve products and services. It takes a proactive culture to constantly push ahead into new areas and ideas. By adopting a continuous improvement mindset, everyone in the organization becomes energized to keep learning about new things. Even subjects that may not be directly tied to the organization's core products and services can lead to useful knowledge.

You never know when someone's seemingly irrelevant learning will help solve a strategic problem down the road.

Employees who are curious and creative are the ones who are are best prepared for today's fast-paced marketplace. They are able to quickly reinvent themselves and their organizations. They do not resist change but relish it! Have you ever noticed that really innovative people are always preparing themselves for the "Next Big Thing" in their lives?

Of the people we've assessed and interviewed—and we're talking about thousands—very few have designs on taking over something or disturbing things. Most are simply driven as lifelong learners and this is something they have always done.

An organization filled with this type of person is better prepared to be successful in the marketplace. And this helps organizations establish their relevance with their customers because they are better prepared to handle all sorts of shifting environments. The ability to adapt quickly to change is essential, about that everyone agrees. An organization that encourages its employees to keep learning is more likely to grow and stay in business.

CASE STUDY:
NATIONAL CONSULTING FIRM LEARNED HOW TO LEVERAGE ITS REPUTATION

A national consulting and training firm asked me to consult on how to better manage their organizational growth. The firm had been making great inroads into national and global corporate clients and was growing fast. The executive management team determined that their firm required a solid strategic platform. The company engaged me to help them build this platform from which to assess its true strengths and weaknesses and to determine how to best leverage them.

Our research showed that although the firm was growing in new client engagements it needed a stronger strategic platform to better support its diverse assignments and related services. The firm was working from a sheet of "one-offs," meaning every engagement had to be tailored for each client. Although that sounded good to clients, it tripled the firm's overhead, because each step had to be planned and implemented on a customized basis.

To fix this problem, the firm needed to reorganize itself into three equal divisions: Training, Consulting and Products, each led by a Client Director with special knowledge for each division. A structured consultative methodology was developed that could be used by all three divisions to cut down the need to reinvent the wheel for each engagement. And a specific hierarchy of training and consulting services was outlined that provided each client with a path of continuous improvement.

These three recommendations were implemented during the first year. We provided consultative support during the next three years, and at the end of the fourth year the firm reported a 250% increase in overall revenues and a commensurate increase in its market relevance.

Best Ways to Build Your Team

Hire staff with wide-ranging interests based on both hard and soft skills. When making a hiring decision, look for prospects who have a track record of learning "new things" — not just one thing. Although this goes against the tradition of hiring people who are specifically trained for the tasks they will need to accomplish, I don't think that's enough anymore. You will probably find many candidates who have long trek records of accomplishments in on specific area. That should get them in the door. But that shouldn't be the whole story. Then find out what else they know and make a decision based on all of the factors.

More important than their technical skills is how

well they adapt to a changing landscape. And will they contribute and work with their team to accomplish its goals? Or will they prefer to silo themselves and work alone? If that is their mindset they won't keep pace when things change — and change certainly happens — and will therefore hold back their group.

During my consulting I often find organizations that have multiple departments or divisions working in silos with little or no care about the others. I learned long ago that you usually receive the behavior you reward, and this simple principle is true with those you supervise, regardless of their level within an organization.

If your organization always hires employees based upon hard skills without consideration for whether they are life-long learners, care about people, want to work with others, and have related soft skills, you will undoubtedly end up with a siloed organization. Each working in their specific area without any motivation to find out what's happening in other areas, or worse, not care. This occurs because the organization has put people into positions who prefer to work alone and has not provided them with an incentive to think or do otherwise.

Treat team members like partners. The most cohesive teams are built on trust for one another and that starts with the team leader. If the leader makes all team members feel like partners by including them in decision-making and seeking their advice, the team will turn on a dime when asked. Being a partner in an organization is far different from being a cog in a big wheel. This is particularly true for a larger organization where it's easier for an employee to sink into the background and not be noticed.

During an engagement with a Fortune 1000 corporation I learned that the engineering division I was working for did not know they had a marketing division in another state they could talk with to gain customer insights.

I realize this sounds hard to believe, but after seven acquisitions and several reorganizations, the company was as fragmented as any I have seen. The project I was assigned had been in progress for 10 years! Not because so much was being developed but because it was virtually impossible to communicate and cooperate with other divisions. No one could gain approval nor cooperation from the other divisions. So the project simply went nowhere. I worked there for nearly a year. After I completed my assignment, I had very little sense of accomplishment. I could only imagine how the employees felt every day.

Build agility into everything you do. The ability to adapt to change is essential. Effective leaders are able to adapt quickly to change. No one can stand still today in the marketplace and expect to be successful. It takes energy to keep things moving forward, but that energy will be well spent. Here are three essentials to leadership and team agility:

1. Clarity of goals and strong communicate skills to reinforce them.
2. Staying on track with goal-oriented tasks.
3. Inspiring team members to be partners in the organization.

Indicator 2: CUSTOMER LOYALTY

Perception versus reality can be quite different. Thoughts and perceptions are built over time by people due to their experiences from a wide variety of sources. People in the organization also hold collective perceptions about the organization and their customers that they have learned over time. This has a direct bearing on an organization's relevance based upon their internal mindset. What is fascinating to me is how different these perceptions can be to those they serve, their customers, and what they really think.

When conducting our Organizational 360°, we often find major gaps between the organization's perception of its performance and its customers' views. We have discovered perception gaps in vital areas have tracked as high as 50% — a dangerously high difference between the two.

This happens when an organization routinely does not place a priority on being informed by its customers' insights, and exclusively attempts to solve its challenges using its internal knowledge. Leaders often feel the need to make quick decisions, because the market moves so fast today, but making them without a full knowledge of their customers' needs can be detrimental. This limits the amount of time a leader will spend seeking input from the organization's most important stakeholder — its customers! As a result, many decisions are made based upon what has worked in the past. Although this is a terrific benchmark to begin an analysis, it's close to flying blind when making a major shift without the market's external advice and counsel.

I admit to having a bias, but after researching over 500 organizations it is clear that organizations that understood their customers' needs and eliminated misperceptions became the leaders in their market. Those that ignored their customers' need because they took too long to determine, or cost too much, often paid a heavy price with declining sales or a major market share loss.

An equally important factor in building customer loyalty is ensuring your product or service portfolio offers a strong connection value to your customers. We live in a crowded market with so many choices its mind-boggling. For example, Amazon is the leading e-retailer in the United States with close to $178 billion US dollars in 2017 net sales. On October 10, 2017, Amazon.com had a total of 598 million products for sale. If you access their website you know that you can spend a significant amount of time looking for different products.

This makes it particularly difficult for lesser-known brands to compete and be "found." People today have so many more choices than ever before. This makes proving relevance all that more important to just stay in business, let alone build customer loyalty. And Amazon is just one of ten major retailers that people can choose from. Walmart, Costco, Walgreens, and many more are all major retailers offering similar products.

So how can an organization build customer loyalty in the age of Amazon's "everything store?" There are several strategies that organizations can use.

Strategy 1: Design a demographics wheel that aligns each of your products or programs to a specific set of demographics such as age, income, education, geography, and related categories that can be sliced and diced according to what your particular product offers.

Strategy 2: Stay clear of a "one product for everyone" approach to your products and services. One size does not fit all! Amazon has a product base of millions that allows its providers to market highly niched products for very specific demographics. For example, a search for "Battery" will turn up dozens of types of batteries for auto, lighting, cameras, and the list goes on. Simply selling batteries is not a product description that can easily be searched online and be found, let alone used to build customer loyalty. But if you market camera batteries for particular types of cameras you have a fighting chance of being found. And you've gotten a customer through your niche offering, you'll want to build their loyalty by providing them with value-added services that no other organization provides.

Strategy 3: Align your messaging with your vision to drive it throughout your organization. You will build a compelling way to heighten customer relationships and loyalty. The path to strong customer loyalty begins with delivering the specific products that they need and being easy to find. Simply making general statements about your product without a direct tie to a customer's specific needs will not prove true value to them.

Strategy 3: Align your messaging with your vision to drive it throughout your organization. You will build a compelling way to heighten customer relationships and loyalty. The path to strong customer loyalty begins with delivering the specific products that they need and being easy to find. Simply making general statements about your product without a direct tie to a customer's specific needs will not prove true value to them.

CASE STUDY:
CHEMICAL MANUFACTURING COMPANY WITH MULTI-GENERATIONAL CHALLENGES

A 100-year old industrial company engaged me to help them make a transition as the baton passed to a new generation. During the discovery mode I found family members fully employed but far from fully engaged. In one case, a team member had been with the company for decades. He would arrive to work at 4:00 AM when no one else was there, punch in, and immediately go into his office to sleep until 8:30 AM when everyone arrived.

I once walked by this person's office in the early afternoon and found him snoring, literally, at his desk. As a senior leader of the company, his behavior created a highly negative culture among the younger employees and reinforced a negative environment.

The message to non-family employees was: We play favorites.

When I brought this to the attention of the CEO I was surprised to learn that not only did he know about the situation, but he told me to "work around it."

Was I able to help the company in many other ways? Sure. But there was no undoing the damage being done by nepotism. I'm afraid in this organization's case the well-known saying was true, "The more things change the more they stay the same." On a positive note, years later, I learned that the company hired a new CEO who, after easing out several of the older family members, was able to lift the company out of the doldrums with a new and inclusive culture.

All organizations need a formalized process by which they can collect critical data from internal and external successes, failures and complaints. The sole purpose of this data is to better understand their customers' needs and how to better serve them. It should never be used within a punitive context to blame or threaten team members for performance lapses or mistakes.

Customers will appreciate the efforts of an organization that pays serious attention to what they say. Determining the root causes of disconnection with them and taking steps to improve services will continue to build strong relevance with them. In fact, when there is clear evidence of this customers will respond with positive communications and stronger loyalty to "their" go-to organization.

You might consider inviting select customers to participate during key planning intervals. This provides customers with the close connection between what they have advised or requested with the updates and changes the organization makes. When they are directly tied to customer suggestions this strengthens their loyalty to the organization and deepens customer satisfaction.

Use customer perception data to find ways to improve.

Nothing is more powerful than taking what a customer has told you and immediately putting a solution into action. Using recently acquired customer perception and satisfaction data, an organization can structure a "Customer Loyalty Program" based upon Recency, Frequency and Monetary valuations to reinforce the organization's continuing value to each of its customers and to drive recurring monthly income. These valuations are designed to build organizational health and growth using both qualitative and quantitative research. This model can be used to determine which customers are the best ones to invest in, including:

- Recency– how recently a customer has

purchased a product from your
organization

- Frequency– how often a customer
  purchases a product from your
  organization

- Monetary– how much a customer spends
  when purchasing a product from your
  organization

When senior executives integrate these three
assessment metrics into decision-making, they can
confidently move forward with new initiatives that
might have taken much longer to evaluate. This
model is best used as a continuous assessment loop.
It leads to improved learning and organizational
growth as well as improved customer loyalty.

CHAPTER SUMMARY

Organization relevance is the result of successfully
building a culture of alignment, integration and
awareness. It is not something that can be purchased
or granted by anyone other than employees of
the organization and satisfied customers. When
an organization consistently meets and exceeds
the expectations of those it serves, it produces
relevance as an attribute of esteem. Someone who

is uninterested in continuous improvement and who does not welcome new ideas or paradigm shifts rarely leads a relevant organization. A fully relevant organization has strong and connected customer relationships and has built into its key offerings strong customer loyalty objectives.

An organization with high relevance scores will have the following:

- Customers of the organization that are highly confident that their needs will be fully met while using this organization.

- Team members who regularly assess and refine its products and services to maintain the highest levels of customer satisfaction.

- Team members who behave and work together with a clear set of objectives that are designed to deliver the highest quality programs and services in their marketplace.

- Team members who are able to describe the organization's top priorities as easily as its most senior executives.

Conclusion:

WHY ORGANIZATIONAL STRATEGY IS SO IMPORTANT FOR DRIVING GROWTH

ALL types of organizations have only four basic drivers: Alignment, Integration, Awareness and Relevance. All else is a supporting point or detail. The central role of these four drivers is to produce value that spurs growth. Value is created by meeting and exceeding customer needs. Therefore, an organization needs to align itself to its top goals and values to drive growth. When these four drivers are continuously implemented organizational growth occurs.

All organizations need to be aware of and keep pace with real world changes and market shifts. It's critical that an organization understands how this saturation of information and quick-paced marketplace affects its customers. The organization must be able to quickly provide customers with solutions to the changing market conditions they experience. Customers value rock solid products and services from organizations that never waiver in their delivery of value. To accomplish this, the organization must understand these essentials to become their customers' trusted source provider.

Once these drivers are fully implemented, the organization is then empowered to capture a percentage of its market by being focused and filtering out distractions while concentrating on driving growth.

Teamwork Makes The Dream Work

Effective leaders need to master three kinds of focus: An outward focus on the needs of its customers, an inward focus on the needs of its employees, and an inward focus to monitor one's own leadership. It's a tall order. Focusing inward on employee needs builds strong teamwork. Focusing outward on customers brings new insights of how to devise strategy, innovate and better manage the organization. Sensitivity to each of these needs when coupled with a razor sharp focus on them strengthens both the leader and team, and drives growth.

And remember: Organizational growth development begins with the customer. A requirement for this development is to balance the organization's strategy with a deep understanding of the target market the organization has identified to serve. Companies have generally been distancing away from large mass markets to market niches offering custom-designed products.

Popular today is the expression, 'market niche' meaning client marketing should be thought of in one-to-one communications. Trying to become larger by offering a huge range of products has fallen out of vogue. This mass approach is counter-intuitive to being able to provide each customer with precisely what they need. Today, targeted market intelligence enables an organization to focus on what they do best and ignore the rest. When this best meets the needs of its customers it builds the organization's value.

Most organizations would like to grow in size, regardless of whether they are large or small. The intensity with which firms pursue growth often depends on how much they have grown in the past. In order to keep pace with their ongoing operating expenses they often pursue growth as a remedy to balance their books. If salaries and related expenses increase without additional income to offset them any organization will need to grow or cut expenses.

There are several ways to produce organizational growth other than adding new clients. These ways could include joint ventures or strategic alliances or an outright merger or acquisition. Although these can create growth faster than an internal organic program, they are less successful in the long run.

They also require new ways to manage relationships and finances that a stand-alone organization does not need.

Given these factors the most successful, and I would argue, scalable organizational growth comes from a strong and cohesive organization that knows how to leverage its combined strength. But simply becoming larger without an effective strategy can be hazardous.

CASE STUDY:
B2B FIRM SEEKS GROWTH

I was engaged by a client who had ventured into a brand new market lacking a defined organizational strategy and solid market data. They had decided to expand beyond their traditional B2B market that they knew like the back of their hand to the consumer market using a five-tier supply chain management. It was complicated and expensive and they lost a lot of money. The cost of expansion had overextended the entire company.

The firm's senior leaders had recognized the new foray would take time and require an investment, but once the six month numbers were reported they sent shockwaves of reality throughout the organization. As time went along the company's senior executives began to question the wisdom of their market expansion and eventually engaged me to help them.

Using our Organizational 360° I immediately concluded they had taken on too much with too little capital to sustain the new market push they had envisioned. They had also suffered some important defections by some of their most productive sales people.

Given all of the factors we gathered, I helped them redraw their goals and strategy.

I made three major recommendations:
1) Narrow the target market to one niche that had the most market traction from their B2B track record.
2) Significantly decrease brand spend.
3) Realign the sales team.

All of our organizational and market development was guided by these three recommendations. After one year the company had stabilized its income to expenses ratio and was breaking even. By the third year the company was turning a healthy profit, and they were a much wiser company.

From my consulting I have concluded that the best growth occurs when it is produced within the capacity of the current organization. The best time to add new resources, new people, and new processes is when growth has occurred, not before. I have watched organizations nearly grow themselves out of business through overly ambitious market expansion plans or when their market unexpectedly turned south.

To Get Ahead You Need To Look Ahead

On the other hand, organizational growth does not take place when its current work takes precedence over new market opportunities. This runs contrary to how growth is achieved. When it comes time to act on new ideas, leadership needs to support them and not allow daily tasks to snuff them out. Nowhere is this more relevant than in an organization that has long-standing products and services that sustained them in year's past.

The four primary drivers discussed in this book –– Alignment, Integration, Awareness and Relevance — provide a solid and sure way to grow any organization. All successful organizations we have researched had all four of these drivers in full operation. They are best practices that work. They are well-researched and time-proven. They allow an organization to look into its future with confidence knowing they will effectively guide them through whatever comes their way. This also makes it easier to get things done because the boundaries of what is most important to an organization's continuing success has been communicated.

A strong leader knows that he or she can't do it all by themselves. It's important to establish a strong leadership team to sustain and scale the business. To get to the next growth stage, the senior leader has to "Let Go" of daily operations and become a coach and equipper — not a doer. This allows the leader to empower those in leadership to lead and multiply what they've learned and pass it along.

Many organizations hit a ceiling in their growth because too many substantial decisions are made by just one or two people. This clogs the organization and often stalls its growth. By expanding the number of decision makers in the organization you expand the number of new ideas that lead to healthy growth.

Rethinking your organization is about aligning what you do best with what your customers want most. That's smart organizational strategy that leads to its health and growth.

QUICK ORGANIZATIONAL HEALTH CHECKUP:

MarketCues makes available a complimentary "Mini-Performance Assessment" that allows you to quickly assess key areas in your organization, including:

- Leadership
- Services
- Branding
- Positioning
- Learning

Our 10-question survey was prepared using our SmartPlan360° Program to give you instant feedback on the health of your organization. This tool should be used as a beginning step to identify key issues in your planning process, not as the basis for your organizational strategy.

FOR BUSINESS:
http://smartplan360program.com

FOR CHURCHES:
http://www.the360churchprogram.com

About the Author

Tom Marin is the founder and president of MarketCues, Inc., a national consulting firm, and is the architect of the SmartPlan360° Program, a software-driven organizational assessment and development program.

Tom has worked for some of the world's largest corporations, nonprofit organizations, educational institutions and churches including First of America Bank, Rand McNally, CNA Insurance Companies, Fuji Photo Film USA, Quebecor Inc., The University of Texas at Austin, Chicago Stock Exchange, Board of Trade Clearing Corporation, London International Financial Futures Exchange, Sydney Futures Exchange, Montreal Futures Exchange, Chicago Board of Options Exchange, Society of Aerospace Engineering, National Entrepreneur Center, The Word Among Us, Ohio Council of Home Care and Hospice, Polk State College, Roper/Whirlpool Corporation, King's Park International Church, Every Nation Churches and Ministries, and Every Nation NYC and NJ Churches.

Tom bases his work on the notion that everyone — no matter their job or level — has the potential to find their leadership skills and leverage them in their every day activities.

About MarketCues, Inc.
www.MarketCues.com

MarketCues, Inc. is a national consulting firm based in Raleigh, NC. The SmartPlan360° Program is the firm's core organizational strategic development tool. What really puts the smarts into our program is how quickly solutions to problems hiding in plain sight are revealed. In traditional coaching and consulting engagements, the first 60 hours or more are spent in the discovery process. The SmartPlan360° Program reduces this time to one hour.

Acknowledgements

I would like to thank my dear friend, Dr. Bert Ghezzi who stood by my side as I put words onto the screen and offered invaluable insights. I would also like to thank my cousin, Pamela Marin, an author and screenwriter, who edited this book.

49278772R00070

Made in the USA
Columbia, SC
20 January 2019